Hom

70 Top Secrets & Tricks To

Beer Brewing Right The First Time:

A Guide To Home Brew Any Beer You Want

With Recipe Journal

By: Jason Scotts

TABLE OF CONTENTS

PUBLISHERS NOTES

Disclaimer

This publication is intended to provide helpful and informative material. It is not intended to diagnose, treat, cure, or prevent any health problem or condition, nor is intended to replace the advice of a physician. No action should be taken solely on the contents of this book. Always consult your physician or qualified health-care professional on any matters regarding your health and before adopting any suggestions in this book or drawing inferences from it.

The author and publisher specifically disclaim all responsibility for any liability, loss or risk, personal or otherwise, which is incurred as a consequence, directly or indirectly, from the use or application of any contents of this book.

Any and all product names referenced within this book are the trademarks of their respective owners. None of these owners have sponsored, authorized, endorsed, or approved this book.

Always read all information provided by the manufacturers' product labels before using their products. The author and publisher are not responsible for claims made by manufacturers.

Paperback Edition

Manufactured in the United States of America

DEDICATION

This book is dedicated to avid drinkers of beer, home brewers and for those who want to start making their own beer.

CHAPTER 1- BEER BREWING BASICS

Before you start making your first beer, you have to at least know what you are trying to do (apart from getting drunk, of course). Since this is your first time to make beer, home brewing is actually an art that has developed over time. At the same time, different brew masters would have different techniques and tips, but feel free to use what is in this book before you experiment on your own.

The process of brewing beer can be broken down into 5 steps, namely:

1. Release the malt sugars by soaking malted barley into hot water.

2. Boil the malt sugar solution with hops for seasoning.

3. Cool that solution and add yeast to start fermentation.

4. During fermentation, the yeast ferments the sugar. The process releases ethyl alcohol and carbon dioxide.

5. Bottle the beer with a little added sugar to get a little carbonation.

Sounds simple, right? Well, it is. However, there are a lot of things that come in between these steps. Don't worry, though; you will learn them as you go by.

Before you shop, here are some terms that you need to keep in mind.

Beer – any kind of beverage made by fermenting malted barley and seasoning with hops

Ale – a kind of beer brewed from a yeast that is top fermenting through a warm and relatively short fermentation.

Attenuation – conversion of sugar to alcohol and CO_2.

Fermentation – there are two parts to this process, which would be referred to as primary and secondary. Overall, these processes would convert malt sugar into beer.

Primary Fermentation – it is where carbon dioxide and Krausen evolves, and where most of the attenuation happens.

Secondary Fermentation – the time where the beer settles and is conditioned before bottling.

Conditioning – a process during secondary fermentation during which the flavors of the final beer are refined. The process continues while the beer is in the bottle.

Hops – these are available in pellets, plugs, or whole. Hop vines may be grown in areas with cool climate, and brewers like you make use of their cone-like flowers.

Wort – solution made out of malt and sugar, which you boil before you ferment.

Priming – the addition of adding fermentable sugar before bottling to give carbonation to the beer.

Krausen – (kroy-zen) the foamy head that forms on top of the beer during fermentation. It is also known as a pro method of priming.

Trub – sediments one can find at the bottom of the fermenter. It is made out of dead yeast and hot or cold break material.

Cold break – these proteins break out of the solution when the wort is cooled quickly and before the yeast is pitched.

Hot break – proteins that clump together and break from the solution while the wort boils

Gravity – just like what you know about density, it is described as the concentration of the malt sugar in the wort.

Specific gravity of water = 1.000 at 59 °F

Gravity of beer wort before fermentation= 1.035 to 1.055

Lager – type of beer brewed from a bottom-fermenting yeast. You can make it by giving a longer and cooler fermentation.

Pitching – addition of yeast to the fermenter.

Racking – the process of siphoning the beer away from the trub, which you would want to do very carefully.

Alpha Acid Units (AAU) – the homebrewing measurement of hops, which has this formula: AAU = weight (in ounces) x percent of Alpha Acids

International Bittering Units (IBU) – easily the more accurate method to measure hops. The formula is: IBU = AAU x wort volume x wort gravity x factors for percent utilization

Zymurgy – the science of brewing and fermentation.

Now that we have all the terms you would most probably encounter when doing home brewing, it's time to hit the stores. You would know more about these terms, and what they actually mean, when you are already in the process.

CHAPTER 2- MAKING YOUR FIRST BREW

This chapter would be your crash course to home brewing, which would make you get acquainted to the entire process of home brewing. Note that you may not know what you are doing exactly during this chapter, but the rest of the book would guide you. In the later parts of the book, you would find out what you have done right, and what you could have done wrong during your practice. Feel free to jump to the next chapters if you want to get explanations right away.

Tip 1: These are the minimum home brew equipment that you need to purchase:

1. Large canning pot, or a brew pot.

2. Glass jar

3. Measuring cup

4. Airlock (You can get it from any homebrew shop.)

5. Fermenter, which can be a food grade plastic bucket, or a glass carboy.

Tip 2: You would want to purchase a glass fermenter, or a stainless one if the glass type isn't available. They are much easier to clean and sterilize, and they provide protection from oxygen leaks, compared to plastic ones that would suffer from oxygen leaks when stored for long periods. Also, plastic containers are difficult to seal, and it would be difficult for you to tell if fermentation has completed.

There is no single rule about how large jars, pots, and buckets should be, but if your space would allow it, consider making long-term purchases. Ideally, you should buy jars that could accommodate 12 ounces or more, and get pots and buckets that would accommodate 5 gallons or more, since most recipes that you would get anywhere would require you to do so. However, buying bigger carboys and glassware would save you a lot of money in the long run.

6. Sanitizer, which would be chlorine bleach or anything that would do the same.

7. A large stirring spoon. It should not be wood.

8. A table spoon

9. Thermometer. It's optional but you might want to get it to control temperature.

10. Bottling bucket or a 6-gallon plastic pail with a spigot and a filling tube. It's optional to get it, but it is highly advisable to buy one to make it easier for you to fill bottles and lessen sediments.

Tip 3: Ingredients may differ, depending on the type of beer that you are going to make. If you have purchased a homebrew kit, you can use that. If you don't have any ingredients yet, go to the nearest homebrew shop and purchase the following.

This list makes a variation of John Palmer's famous Cincinnati Pale Ale, which makes 5 gallons. Take note that this beer is the American version of the English pale ale, and it is known for being slightly bitterer and less fruity than a lot of European beers. Most brewers advise this to be the first batch to make, but you can adjust the ingredients depending on what's available in your neighborhood home brew store.

3-4 lbs. Pale Unhopped Malt Extract syrup – brew shops normally call this UME. This would be the ingredient that would give your beer much of its color, so you may want to ask the store you are buying from to give you a UME appropriate for pale beer. However, it's okay if you purchase a darker UME.

2-3 lbs. Sparkling Amber dried malt extract

12 AAU Simcoe bittering hops, or any other hop variety.

2.5 ounces of Cascade finishing hops (You can actually use any variety you want.)

Tip: You may want to buy pellet hops. They are easier to find in the stores, and they are convenient to use for first-time brewing.

2 packs of dried ale yeast

Tip 4: You may see that the hops in the store are being measured in AAUs or HBUs which are standard bittering units of measurements for home brews. If you have 4 oz of an 8% alpha acid hop, that would equal to 32 AAUs. Alpha acid is that thing that makes your beer taste bitter, and if you need to figure out how much hop you are going to need for the recipe, simply divide the recipe's AAU by the AA percentage on your hops (In this example, that is just 32 divided by 8, which gives you 4.). You can also take note of usual AAs for most hops available.

Preparation

1. Gather the ingredients. Bring out your brewing kit or the ingredients listed above.

2. Boil a certain amount of water for sterilizing needs.

Tip 4: You are going to need to have at least one gallon of water (sterilized) for a lot of minor tasks. Boil the water, and let it cool afterwards. Cover the container and keep in room temperature.

3. See to it that you have sanitized (not just cleaned) your equipment. Here's a very important rule when it comes to brewing beer – the cleanliness of your equipment would be a factor in the quality of your beer, so make sure that you keep everything clean. You can use mild, unscented detergent to clean everything, and make sure that you rinse it well.

Tip 5: You can create a sanitizing solution by mixing water and chlorine bleach. The ideal concentration would be 1 tablespoon of bleach for every gallon of water. After you have soaked all other tools in this mix, you can rinse them using the water you boiled previously. However, you can also use cheap vodka to sanitize your tools if you do not have time to prepare a solution and rinse afterwards.

Making Wort

This would be the exciting part. The wort is the term that most brewers call the sweet-tasting, amber-looking fluid that one extracts from the malted barley. The yeast would later ferment this into beer. Here's how to make it:

1. Bring the brew water to a boil.

Bring 2 gallons of water to a boil into the brew pot. Place the boiled water into the fermenter and leave it there to cool. Next, bring 3 gallons of water to a boil in the brew pot. Take note that you will be boiling all of the extract that you have in the 3 gallons and then add this concentrated wort to the 2 gallons of water sitting in your fermenter.

Tip 6: If your beer kit or recipe requires you to add some specialty grain, you would need to crush (or mash), and then steep the grains before you add the extract.

2. Rehydrate the dried yeast.

Tip 7: Some people do not do this part and still get the results that they want, but doing this process would yield far superior results.

While waiting for the brew water to boil, take out the two packs of dried ale yeast. Put 1 cup of warm, pre-boiled water (35-40°C or 95-105°F) in a sanitized jar and then add the yeast. Stir, and cover the jar with plastic wrap. Wait for 15 minutes.

The next step is to "proof" the yeast. Add one tsp. of malt extract (If you don't have this, you can use table sugar instead.) to a small amount of water (That can be ¼ cup.) and boil to sanitize. Let the sugar solution to cool and then add it to the yeast jar you prepared earlier. Cover it and place in a warm area away from direct sunlight.

Tip 8: Check the jar after 30 minutes – it should look like it is foaming or churning. If it looks like everything is at the bottom of the jar, it's probably dead. When that happens, repeat the procedure, but add more yeast.

3. Add the malt extract. When the water in the brew pot is boiling, turn off the heat and add the malt extract. Make sure that your extract is completely dissolved (If it's the dry variety, see to it that you do not see any clumps, and if it's the syrup kind, make sure that none of it is sticking to the bottom of the pot.).

Turn the heat back on and let it boil.

Tip 9: To avoid scorching, make sure that you stir the wort regularly while it's boiling. Watch it carefully to ensure that it won't burn.

4. Add the hops.

Tip 10: If your brewing kit comes with unhopped extract, add the bittering hop addition. Use a timer and boil the wort for an hour.

5. Watch out for the boil overs. Boil overs for beginners are the worst part, as it would create a mess and lessen the amount of beer that you can make. While the wort is boiling, you will see that foam forms on the top of the entire mix.

Tip 11: Make sure that you watch it and stir frequently to prevent boil overs. Turn the heat down and blow on it when needed. You can also spray cold water over the brew pot when the foam starts to rise.

Tip 12: You can drop a few copper pennies into the pot to prevent boil overs.

6. Throw in finishing hops (optional). Perform this step if you have unhopped malt extract, or you want additional character to your hopped extract.

Tip 12: Make sure that you add the finishing, or any additional hops during the latter part of the wort boil. For this recipe, add them during the last 15 minutes of the boil.

7. Turn off the heat.

Tip 13: The time you need to spend on boiling would depend on two factors: the "hot break," which happens in step 5, and boiling if you need to add hops. That would actually depend on the recipe that you are doing, but you would want to remember this as you would want to experiment later on.

Tip 14: If you are using hopped extract and you plan to not use any additional hops, you would only need to boil through the hot break stage to get the protein on the beer, which would be about 15 minutes. If you are using hopped malt extract, but you need to add aroma hops or flavoring, you would probably want to boil around 30 minutes. As the hot break is usually marked by the foaming on the surface of the boil, take note that with some variants of extract, the hot break may not be as foamy as this recipe.

8. Cool the wort. Make sure that you would be able to cool the wort to the appropriate yeast pitching temperature (For ale yeast, temperature should be 18 to 32°C or 65 to 90°F.) as quickly as you can. Use a thermometer to be sure about the temperature.

Tip 15: You would need to prepare a cold water bath, and immerse the boiling pot in it. You can use your sink, a large metal basin, or even your bathtub for the bath. Make sure that you put on the pot's lid to prevent getting cold water or contaminants into your wort.

Fermentation

If you are planning to be a master brewer in the future, you have to appreciate this science as early as now. In addition, this provides you the skill to tell onlookers what is happening to your beer from 10 feet away, including what process is taking place. To ferment your beer, here are the steps:

1. Pitch the prepared yeast.

Take out the rehydrated yeast you prepared earlier and put it in the fermentation bucket.

2. Add the wort.

Dump the cooled wort in the fermentation bucket in such a way that it splashes around and swirls the mix in the vessel. When you do so, the action adds oxygen to the mix which the yeast needs for its growth. This would be that one time that you want to do this kind of transfer for the beer to be exposed to oxygen to get the yeast activated for fermentation. All the other transfers that you would do would have to be done "quietly" with a siphon to prevent oxygenation.

Tip 16: If you have added additional hops during the wort boil, you can remove them during this part using a strainer. However, you can opt not to take them off the mix if you want to.

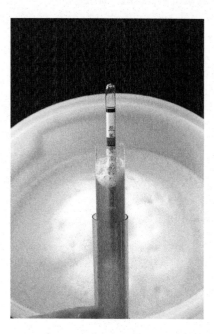

3. Move the Fermenter to a Secure Location

With the lid on, store the fermenter in a safe location for two weeks.

Tip 17: Your storage should have a temperature of 65-70°F or 18-21°C. Since you used ale yeast, the storage can be warmer, but only up to 75°F or 24°C. Any warmer than that, or if the temperature exceeds 80 °F or 26 °C, the flavor of the beer might be affected. As soon as you are done moving the fermenter, put in the airlock to prevent extra oxygen from getting into the beer.

Tip 18: You might get excited when you see that the airlock is bubbling after 24 hours, which is evidence that fermentation is taking place. This would happen for the next 2-4 days, if the conditions for fermenting the yeast were properly met. The activity would diminish as the yeast eats up the malt sugars, but the yeast would still ferment the beer even if the bubbling decreases. No matter what it looks like, leave the fermenter alone for two weeks.

4. Clean Your Equipment

Wash the boiling pot and other items that you have used. Make sure that you only use mild detergents, preferably unscented, to prevent damaging and getting unwanted smells onto your aluminum tools.

Bottling

After two weeks, it's time to reap your rewards by bottling the good stuff. Here are the things that you are going to need:

1. 48 12oz. bottles

2. Bottle brush – you can use the house cleaning or the kitchen variety

3. Bottle capper

4. Bottling bucket

5. Racking cane or bottle filler or siphon

6. Sugar, 4-5 oz.

Steps:

1. Prepare the bottles.

Tip 19: Most 5-gallon batches would require 2 cases of bottles (Use 12 oz. ones.). Generally, you can use any bottles that you like, as long as you clean and sanitize them before filling them up. If you are going to recycle old bottles, make sure that they do not have dirt or mold deposits. Scrub them with the bottle brush, then sanitize.

2. Do the same for the bottle caps.

Tip 20: The best way to clean them is to use a sanitizing solution, which is just like the one you used in the fermenting bucket. If you are going to use Groelsch-style caps, you can clean the ceramic part with the bottles. If you are using rubber seals, you can sanitize them using the same sanitizing solution you made for your equipment.

3. Prepare the priming sugar.

The priming sugar is made by doing the following:

Boil ¾ cup (or 4 oz.) of corn sugar. If you are going to use cane sugar for the solution, you can dissolve 2/3 cups of sugar into 2 cups and water, and then boil the mix in a pan.

4. Put priming sugar into the beer. After taking the pan off the heat, cover it and let it cool.

Find a container that is the same size as your fermenting bucket. Make sure that it is cleaned and sanitized. Put the priming sugar solution in it. Gently transfer the beer from the fermenter into this container. You can use a siphon to make it easier.

Tip 21: Do not simply pour the beer – you wouldn't want it to splash and get oxygen in it, which would cause massive quality issues. If you want to mix it thoroughly with the priming sugar, put the siphon in the lower part of the container, and gently let the beer swirl to mix with the solution.

Tip 22: If you do not want to get a bottling bucket, pour the priming solution instead into the fermenter and gently stir it. Let the sediments settle for about 30 minutes before you proceed to filling your bottles.

5. Bottle.

Fill the bottles with beer, place the sanitized bottle cap, and crimp it using the bottle capper. If you want to save time and prevent oxygen and bacteria from getting into your beer, it would be wise to let someone else do the capping.

6. Store

Store the bottles out of direct light in room temperature for two weeks to allow them to carbonate.

Tip 23: The bottles will have a thin layer of yeast on the bottom. That's normal, so don't worry about it. It would not affect the taste or quality of your beer.

CHAPTER 3- A FEW TIPS ON BREWING

The previous chapter essentially covered everything that you need when it comes to making home brews, but of course, you are aiming to do it like a pro. The following chapters would cover everything that you need to make your home brew taste just as good as your favorite beer.

Essentially, making the best home brews would be about being able to do the exact thing over and over again, and not believing in sheer luck. A lucky brewer would be any person that can create the best beer he has ever tasted, but not necessarily be able to do it again. The secret to being a pro brewer is record keeping, and being able to do all the brewing steps in an orderly fashion.

At the same time, it also pays to experiment, especially if you are trying to create your own unique flavor. However, it pays to master one type of beer first before moving on to a more complicated process.

In addition, keep in mind that consistency and cleanliness are the keys to making more batches that are successful. It does not mean that you should aim for perfection all the time – you may expect to fail especially if you are experimenting to make your own unique beer. However, make sure that if you have created your first successful beer, you keep a record of everything that you have done in an orderly fashion. Also, keep in mind that 75% of the time, the most successful beers are created using clean equipment and bottles. Hence, make sure that you pay attention that no contaminant enters your brew.

CHAPTER 4- CLEAN EQUIPMENT IS ESSENTIAL

There are a number of ways that you can keep your equipment clean, and when it comes to brewing beer, there are only a few ways to keep in mind when it comes to cleanliness and sanitation. For starters, here is a checklist to be able to memorize which should be just washed and which should be sterilized.

Clean

• Brew Pot

• Stirring Spoon

Clean and Sanitize

• Tablespoon

• Measuring Cup

• Yeast Starter Jar

• Fermenter and Lid

• Air Lock

Here are a number of tips and tricks to make sure that you have the cleanest equipment, and they all came from the pros.

Tip 24: You can use cheap vodka as sanitizer in the fermenter – it instantly kills any insects that may come and breach the airlock. You can also keep some of it in a midsize spray bottle, and you can spray some in your glass carboy before you pitch the yeast. Save some in the spray bottle so you have it handy when you do not have time to prepare.

Tip 25: Some home brewers discourage using bleach to sanitize equipment, because chlorine and maltose combined equals to bad flavor. Should you ever want to still use bleach, make sure that you rinse it well or use mild and odorless sanitizers instead.

Tip 26: You can sanitize all your bottles at once by using a large cooler and completely submerging the bottles in a solution of water and no-rinse sanitizer. Make sure that the bottles are completely submerged, and let them soak until you are ready to bottle.

Tip 27: If you are cleaning aluminum and stainless steel, do not use bleach. Use mild detergents or percarbonate-based cleaners instead to avoid corrosion.

CHAPTER 5- BEER KITS, BEER SUGAR & MALT EXTRACT

About Beer Kits

Here is one thing you should really remember. Beer production is a straightforward process, and you probably would not need to buy beer kits at all. The first beer that you would probably fail making at home is the one that you got from a bad beer kit you purchased from the grocery store.

Do not take it the wrong way. Some beer kits can make beer that you can actually drink, but you are trying to avoid adulterated beer. Pay attention to these tips should you want to use these kits:

Tip 28: Do not believe the instruction that you should add cane or corn sugar.

Tip 29: Do not use the yeast that came with the kit, unless its expiration date is still far away or the yeast is from a brand you can trust. The reason is that the yeast may be old or exposed to harsh shipping conditions. To begin with, it may be bad yeast.

In short, if you are going to use beer kits, just follow the instructions and tips in this book. That way, you can avoid making sparkly pond water that you would never want to drink.

It may also be wise to buy beer kits that you can purchase from trusted home brewers. They generally produce better tasting ones compared to commercial bag packs. Quality home brew kits tend to taste better than most commercial beers.

Tip 30: If you can't find a good home brew shop in your area, you can create your own kit. Here's what you need for 5 gallons of beer:

5-7 pounds of hopped pale extract syrup, with original gravity (OG) of 1.038 to 1.053

1-2 ounces of hops (This is for more hop character, if you want to have more of it.)

2 packs of dry ale yeast. Add 1 more for backup.

¾ cup of corn sugar for bottle priming

Shopping for Malt Extracts

The quality of freshness in the extract is very important, and the old ones would most probably have stale, blunt, or even soapy taste. What causes it is the oxidation of the acid compounds in the malt. When shopping for extracts, you may want dry malt extract instead – they have better shelf lives.

Extracts are commonly available in dark, amber, or pale, and can be bought as either hopped or unhopped. The hopped ones usually have mild to moderate bitterness. Wheat malt extracts, on the other hand, are also available to tailor to specific beer tastes that you want.

Tip 31: It may also be wise to shop according to brand. I would recommend Munton & Fison, John Bull, Ireks, Edme, Mountmellick, Alexander's, and Cooper's.

CHAPTER 6- BEER & WATER

Water is one of the most important ingredients in beer; after all, this drink is mostly water. Different kinds of water can affect the taste of beer, and that is why there are types of water that are ideal for brewing. You have probably heard about the soft water of Pilsen and the pure Rocky Mountain spring water, which are not known because of their location, but the beer they make.

The minerals found in the water you use can create a difference in the starch conversion of the mash you are using. However, once the sugars are being produced during the process, the effect of water lessens on the flavor.

Tip 32: Should you doubt which type of water you should use, there's only one simple rule: if the water tastes great, the beer would taste awesome. For your first beer, you may want to use bottled water instead of tap water.

Tip 33: There are also some odors in water that would disappear when you are boiling it, but watch out for sediments. If it tastes bad, don't use it. Also, don't think about adding salts unless it is intended in the recipe.

CHAPTER 7- BEER & HOPS

So, how does one choose the right hops for a beer? There are hundreds of hops available, and that would be depending on the type of beer that you are trying to make.

Brewers also debate on the form of hop that they should buy. As discussed in the first chapter, hops come as whole, plug, or pellets.

Tip 34: If you are shopping for hops, here are the pros and cons when shopping for each type:

Whole

Pros: They float and it is easy to remove them from the wort. They also give out the best aroma, and they have the best form for dry hopping.

Cons: They soak up a lot of wort, and you wouldn't want to lose some of the wort after the boil. They are also harder to weigh for accuracy.

Plug

Pros: They are fresher for a longer time, and they behave like whole hops during the wort boil. They are also more convenient to measure.

Cons: They still soak up the wort, and they are difficult to use when you need measures other than half-ounce increments.

Pellets

Pros: Easy to store and easy to weigh, and they don't soak up the wort.

Cons: They form sludge in the wort and they may be difficult to strain. It's difficult to add dry hop with it, and it gives off less aroma.

Tip 34: No matter what kind or form of hop you are going to use, it is very important to use the fresh ones. The old ones would turn brown, and may give off a pungent smell like that of old cheese.

Tip 35: It is best to have hops stored in a cool, dry place, where it would be protected from oxygen. It's also a good rule to follow when buying hops – oxygenated hops that are merely stored in thin plastic bags would lose 50% of their bitterness in a few months.

Categories of Hops

You may hear about these categories in forums or in some homebrew discussion. You know already about bittering hops, but there are other categories that other home brewers like to purchase. They are used both for bittering and finishing, and you may want to experiment with these hop types in the future.

Aroma hops, just like how the name implies, give off good smell for the beer, and those who use it like it for its fine, cleaner profile.

Noble hops are famous for having the best aroma, and they are mostly grown in Europe. They are mostly recognized for being used in lager-type beers, but it is purely tradition.

Tip 36: You can use noble hops even if you are brewing ale, or other beer types. In addition, there is no strict rule on which type of hops to use in a particular type of beer. Most of the time, it would depend on how you would like your beer to taste.

Tip 37: If you are gunning for a traditional recipe, or you are trying to make your own version of a popular beer, home brewing sites and forums would be extremely helpful in finding the hops used in most popular beer recipes.

CHAPTER 8- SPECIALTY GRAINS FOR YOUR BEER

If you want to brew a batch of beer using specialty grains, you do not need to use additional equipment. You just need a sock, or a grain bag, that you would use in seeping or mashing the grains. You can add the grains even when you are trying to brew malt extracts, which provides extra flavor and character to the beer. Well, most of the award-winning beers around the world are made using specialty grains and their combinations.

Tip 38: There are grains that need to be mashed first, and some would just need to be crushed inside the bag and it's ready for steeping. Find out from the seller about the type of grain you are buying to know what you need to do first before you but the bag of grains in hot water.

Steeping looks like and feels like making tea. Seeping the grains too long in hot water would result in tannin extraction, and would give out a dry taste, just like black tea.

Tip 39: Some books say that you can boil the grains right in the pot and then they can be strained out. Try to avoid this because it would most certainly lead to tannin extraction, or that tea-like quality in your beer, which would give it a dry taste. Another drawback of doing this is that it makes the grains lose much of their flavor.

CHAPTER 9- BEER & YEAST

Yeast are well, live organisms that live in order to ferment your beer. Essentially, there are two kinds of yeast that you can choose: ale and lager. Ale yeasts are those yeasts that perform the fermentation at the top of the fermenter while the lager does the opposite. Ale yeasts would also like warmer temperatures, and would go dormant if the temperature falls below 55°F. Lager yeasts would do their job even if the temperature falls to 40°F.

Tip 40: You can purchase yeast in two product forms, dry and liquid, but for convenience's sake, use the dry variant instead. Dry yeast is easier to store, and you can rehydrate it when you are ready to use it.

Tip 41: If you are trying to brew beer at home, consider the space that you have for storage. Temperature will play a huge role in deciding which type of beer you would be able to make, without having to spend for a cellar for controlled fermenting temperature. If you live in an area with high temperature, it would always be safe to brew ale beers.

Tip 42: When fermenting, never solely rely on the amount of foam that you see in the airlock. That is highly unreliable when you are determining the level of fermentation, and would make you think that no activity is happening, or fermentation is done. To be sure, always have a hydrometer, which would gauge the fermentation.

Tip 43: If you live in an area where there is high temperature for most of the year, it may be possible to control the temperature in your fermenter to make it more suitable for the type of beer that you want to make. One trick is to always have PET bottles filled with water frozen in your refrigerator. You can put them around the fermenter if you need colder temperature for certain beers. Of course, always have your thermometer handy.

Yeast Strains

There are a lot of yeast strains to choose from, and just like how it works with hops, they work according to the beer type that you are working on. Belgian strains, for example, would give off that trademark fruity smell, while the German strains produce strong clove smells. Certain breweries also produce strains for distinct beer quality and taste. If you are looking forward to acquiring certain flavor and aroma, you may want to acquire yeasts according to maker.

Tip 44: Resources for yeast strains are also found in numerous home brewery sites and forums. If you are gunning for a certain beer taste, texture, or aroma, brewer sites and forums or home brewery shops would be able to tell you which type of strain is used for a particular recipe.

Tip 45: If you are going to experiment with yeast, you would have to mind what effects they are going to give your beer. Some yeast strains imitate certain beer fermentation problems, so you might want to avoid such strains first.

Tip 46: When brewing beer, pay attention to fermentation and yeast strains, as different types of beers would require different methods when it comes to fermenting and activating the yeast. If you want to try making a lager beer as your first beer, try using strains that would yield clean and lager-like taste, even if you were fermenting at ale temperature. Kölsch yeast would make an excellent choice.

CHAPTER 10- BREWING YOUR BEER

Now that you know how to boil the wort, it's time to be acquainted with the processes. When it comes to beer, there's such a thing as a good and bad boil.

Tip 47: If the foam rises and forms a smooth surface, it's a good boil. If the foam suddenly goes to the side and produces billows, that's a boil over and that is bad. The wort is about to spill over, and you will lose some of it.

You have read in an earlier chapter something about the hot break, which is that 5-20 minutes during the boil wherein the proteins clump together, and to you it looks like something you would see in egg drop soup. When adding hops, wait for this to happen, and begin timing the boil.

Tips and Tricks to Boiling and Cooling

Tip 48: If you cover the pot, make sure that you watch it like a hawk. Covering the pot is the quickest way to get a boil over, which you are trying to avoid.

Tip 49: Once the wort is boiling, do not cover the pot, or only cover it partially. Sulfur compounds evolve during the boil, and you are trying to let them evaporate. If not, they would give off a corn or cooked cabbage flavor to the beer.

Tip 50: Cold break is very important, as you would need to create a thermal shock to some proteins in order for them to precipitate out of the wort. If you do not quickly cool the wort after boiling, the beer would create a Chill Haze, a type of cosmetic problem in the beer. A hazy beer also becomes stale faster than the non-hazy ones.

Tip 51: You can either use a cold water bath or an ice bath to cool the wort. Some people actually put ice directly to the cooling wort. Well, this works as long as the ice is clean. Do not use commercial ice, since they most probably have dormant bacteria, which will spoil the beer. Also, even if you are not going to directly put ice into the wort (e.g. using a frozen plastic bottle), make sure that you sanitize the outside of the bottle first.

Tip 52: Most first-time brewers complain about too much bitterness in their beer. Most of the time, the reason for an over-bittered beer is because brewers read the boiling time in the recipe wrong. If your recipe says that the boil time for hops is 60 minutes, 20 minutes, or 15 minutes, it does not mean that you have to boil the wort with the hops in it for 95 minutes. The 20 minutes and 15 minutes would mean points in the ball time when you should add the hops.

Tip 53: In the future, you may opt to purchase wort chillers, which would be extremely efficient if you are cooling volume boils that are too heavy and hazardous to carry to the sink or bathtub.

Tip 54: Hook up a hose to the wort chiller before you place the pot. This would protect your face from the extremely hot steam when you put the pot into the chiller.

CHAPTER 11- TRANSFERRING, BOTTLING & CHILLING

Transferring the beer from one vessel to another is a tricky thing because you do not want to get the wort to be oxidized the wrong way. There is one rule about getting oxygen: you would only want it when you are pitching the yeast, and you should prevent it from getting into the wort afterwards. Oxygen leads to a cardboard-like taste in the beer, and it also promotes the growth of beer-spoiling bacteria. Apart from preventing oxidation, you should also make sure that everything that touches the wort after it has cooled are thoroughly sanitized.

Tip 55: When you are racking or bottling the beer, do not start a siphon by sucking on it. You will contaminate the batch with bacteria on your mouth. Remember that all parts of the siphon should be sanitized before using it to transfer the beer into the bottle.

Tip 56: To make sure that it is clean, leave the siphon full of sanitizer, and place the racking cane in your beer. Release the clamp or valve and let the sanitizer drain into a jar or a vessel. Make sure that the siphon outlet is lower than the fermenter, or you will get sanitizer into your beer. To be sure, make use of no-rinse sanitizer or vodka. When the sanitizer is completely drained, the siphon will start drawing out the beer.

Tip 57: If you do not have a bottling bucket, use a sanitized bucket with a spigot so that you would not have to siphon the beer.

CHAPTER 12- TROUBLESHOOTING YOUR BEER

Here's the bad news about making your own beer: it is easy to spoil it, and it would require extra diligence to make sure that you do not contaminate it. At the same time, there are a lot of things that you can only learn through experience, because processes may turn out differently.

However, there are only three things that are probably the cause of some beer damage if you have a good recipe and quality ingredients. These are wrong temperature, bad yeast, and poor or inadequate sanitation. Making sure that you avoid these would get you a better chance in having a good beer.

At the same time, keep in mind that when it comes to brewing beer for the first time, it is possible that your first batch may have an odd aroma or taste, but it is very likely that it is still drinkable (depending on certain conditions, of course). So if you think that there is something about your first beer, and if you are wondering if it is ruined, the most probable answer is No.

Here's one great tip: you would most likely notice that there is something wrong with the beer when the batch is already in the fermenter. The first worry that you might have is when you think that there is no fermentation or there is some strange activity happening. However, there would be a lot of times when the remedy for this is to actually the beer leave alone.

Here are some troubleshooting tips if you feel that your batch is not turning out the way you expect.

Tip 58: If you suspect that fermentation did not happen, here are the things that probably happened:

1. Wort too hot (The yeast was killed, or stunned.)

2. Wort too cold (caused the yeast to be dormant)

3. Fermentation is already complete (Look out for a ring of crud-like substance inside the fermenter.)

4. You put too little yeast.

5. Fermentation works, but you did not seal the bucket completely, so you can't see bubbles in airlock. Solution: use a hydrometer to monitor fermentation.

Tip 59: If you see that there is no activity in the fermenter after two days, you can opt to alter the temperature and see if it would make a difference. If you believe that the yeast was killed, you can pitch the yeast again under a more favorable condition.

Tip 60: If you are doing the recipe again and the fermentation was fine before, but when you did it again, nothing happened or something strange is happening in the fermenter, the best way to identify the problem is to wait until the fermentation time is done. It is probable that the yeast you are using has different quality or has less vigor than the one you previously used. You would only have something to worry about if the beer has strange odor or taste after it has been conditioned.

Tip 61: If there is a puckering, tea-like quality to the beer that seems bitter (astringency) and you used malt extract, the grains are probably steeped in too much water, or you used more than 3 quarts of water per pound of grain. The steeping water may also be too hot, or it is over 170 °F.

Tip 62: If the beer smells like bananas, you may have used Belgian strain of yeast. If this is not what you want, consider using other yeast strains instead. Also, it is possible that the fermentation temperature is too high, which most likely affects lager-type yeasts. It is also possible that you made an error in the pitching rate.

Tip 63: If the beer is too sour, or it tastes like tart, it may be because you used raspberries or other ingredients that would give that flavor. If you didn't, the beer is contaminated.

Tip 64: If the wort is too dark, it probably burned or it is too concentrated. You may be able to still fix it by adding more water during the boil.

Tip 65: If there is too little foam, it's possible that the fermentation is weak, or your fermenter is dirty. It's also possible that something went wrong during the hot break, which leads to too little protein in the wort.

Tip 66: If you suspect that there are molds on the surface of the beer, check the beer if that is yeast. If that's the case, do not worry about it. But if those are molds, it's likely that the wort is exposed to too much oxygen while you are bottling the beer.

Tip 67: If there are too many sediments in your bottled beer, you may want to let the beer fall clear first before bottling it next time. Sediments in home brew beer are normal, and it won't affect the taste.

Tip 68: If the beer smells like solvent, or something close to the smell of nail polish, the original gravity of the beer is too high. It's also possible that it has too little air, or the fermentation temperature is too high.

Tip 69: If the beer tastes like it has too much carbon, it's possible that it is contaminated. The over-carbonation may also be because you put too much priming sugar, or the beer did not mix well with the priming solution.

Tip 70: If the beer tastes flat even after it was bottle-conditioned, it is possible that you forgot to add the priming sugar before bottling, or that the beer and the priming sugar did not mix adequately. You might want to consider storing the bottles to a warmer condition. It is also possible that the beer needs more time to be conditioned.

Tip 71: If the beer shows slimy strands, that's a telltale sign of lacto infection. Throw it away.

Tip 72: If the bottled beer shows a milky layer at the top, and there are residues at the sides of the bottle neck, your beer suffered from microderm infection. That beer would smell rotten and it would have a nasty taste.

Note: Do not confuse this with dew formation near the bottle cap, or protein ring at the top of the bottle. These are normal. Smell the beer first so that you won't have to throw it away, in any case.

Tip 73: If the beer smells sweet, as in like molasses, there is acetic infection in the beer. That means the beer is turning into malt vinegar, which tastes good, but of course, that is not what you intend to do.

Tip 74: If the beer has a cardboard or sherry-like taste to it, it means that the beer has been oxidized too much. Drink the beers as soon as you can, because they will expire earlier than you expect.

Tip 75: If the beer smells like cat musk or is skunky, it has been exposed to light. Use darker bottles next time. You can still drink them, if you can tolerate the smell.

CHAPTER 13- GETTING BETTER BY TASTE TESTING

If you think that you did a great job on your first beer, the only way to find out is to have someone else taste it. Also, being a pro would entail being able to do it again, and also being able to add a certain twist to the same recipe.

Tip 76: Always make sure that you not only follow procedure, but also get feedback. You will be able to make sure that you do everything correctly by having a brewer's log and being able to document how you followed the procedures each time you do a recipe or use a beer kit again. That would allow you to use the same notes that you have, but also be able to make your next batches taste a little differently. Of course, you would be able to know if you made an excellent variation if you let someone else sample it.

Tip 77: There is something great about free beer, especially if you are the one who made it. Throwing a party is a great way to find a lot of people to taste your brew and get the feedback that you need.

RECIPE JOURNAL

RECIPE #1

RECIPE: _____

Ingredients:

- ....
- ....
- ....
- ....
- ....
- ....
- ....
- ....

- ....
- ....
- ....
- ....
- ....
- ....
- ....
- ....

Directions:

....

....

....

....

....

....

....

....

....

....

....

....

....

....

Preparation Time: **Servings:**

RECIPE #2

RECIPE: _____

Ingredients:

- .... - ....
- .... - ....
- .... - ....
- .... - ....
- .... - ....
- .... - ....
- .... - ....
- .... - ....

Directions:

....

....

....

....

....

....

....

....

....

....

....

....

....

Preparation Time: **Servings:**

RECIPE #3

RECIPE: _____

Ingredients:

- ....
- ....
- ....
- ....
- ....
- ....
- ....
- ....

- ....
- ....
- ....
- ....
- ....
- ....
- ....
- ....

Directions:

....

....

....

....

....

....

....

....

....

....

....

....

....

Preparation Time: **Servings:**

RECIPE #4

RECIPE: _____

Ingredients:

- ....
- ....
- ....
- ....
- ....
- ....
- ....
- ....

- ....
- ....
- ....
- ....
- ....
- ....
- ....
- ....

Directions:

....

....

....

....

....

....

....

....

....

....

....

....

....

....

....

Preparation Time: **Servings:**

RECIPE #5

RECIPE: _____

Ingredients:

- ....
- ....
- ....
- ....
- ....
- ....
- ....
- ....

- ....
- ....
- ....
- ....
- ....
- ....
- ....
- ....

Directions:

....

....

....

....

....

....

....

....

....

....

....

....

....

Preparation Time: **Servings:**

RECIPE #6

RECIPE: _____

Ingredients:

- ....
- ....
- ....
- ....
- ....
- ....
- ....
- ....

- ....
- ....
- ....
- ....
- ....
- ....
- ....
- ....

Directions:

....

....

....

....

....

....

....

....

....

....

....

....

....

....

....

....

Preparation Time: **Servings:**

RECIPE #7

RECIPE: _____

Ingredients:

- · ....
- · ....
- · ....
- · ....
- · ....
- · ....
- · ....
- · ....

- · ....
- · ....
- · ....
- · ....
- · ....
- · ....
- · ....
- · ....

Directions:

....

....

....

....

....

....

....

....

....

....

....

....

....

Preparation Time: **Servings:**

RECIPE #8

RECIPE: _____

Ingredients:

- ....
- ....
- ....
- ....
- ....
- ....
- ....
- ....

- ....
- ....
- ....
- ....
- ....
- ....
- ....
- ....

Directions:

....

....

....

....

....

....

....

....

....

....

....

....

....

....

Preparation Time: **Servings:**

RECIPE #9

RECIPE: _____

Ingredients:

- ....
- ....
- ....
- ....
- ....
- ....
- ....
- ....

- ....
- ....
- ....
- ....
- ....
- ....
- ....
- ....

Directions:

....

....

....

....

....

....

....

....

....

....

....

....

....

Preparation Time: **Servings:**

RECIPE #10

RECIPE: _____

Ingredients:

- ....
- ....
- ....
- ....
- ....
- ....
- ....
- ....

- ....
- ....
- ....
- ....
- ....
- ....
- ....
- ....

Directions:

....

....

....

....

....

....

....

....

....

....

....

....

....

....

....

....

Preparation Time: **Servings:**

RECIPE #11

RECIPE: _____

Ingredients:

- ....
- ....
- ....
- ....
- ....
- ....
- ....
- ....

- ....
- ....
- ....
- ....
- ....
- ....
- ....
- ....

Directions:

....

....

....

....

....

....

....

....

....

....

....

....

....

....

....

....

Preparation Time: **Servings:**

RECIPE #12

RECIPE: _____

Ingredients:

- ....
- ....
- ....
- ....
- ....
- ....
- ....
- ....

- ....
- ....
- ....
- ....
- ....
- ....
- ....
- ....

Directions:

....

....

....

....

....

....

....

....

....

....

....

....

....

....

....

....

Preparation Time: **Servings:**

RECIPE #13

RECIPE: _____

Ingredients:

- ....
- ....
- ....
- ....
- ....
- ....
- ....
- ....

- ....
- ....
- ....
- ....
- ....
- ....
- ....
- ....

Directions:

....

....

....

....

....

....

....

....

....

....

....

....

....

Preparation Time: **Servings:**

RECIPE #14

RECIPE: _____

Ingredients:

- ....
- ....
- ....
- ....
- ....
- ....
- ....
- ....

- ....
- ....
- ....
- ....
- ....
- ....
- ....
- ....

Directions:

....

....

....

....

....

....

....

....

....

....

....

....

....

....

Preparation Time: **Servings:**

RECIPE #15

RECIPE: _____

Ingredients:

- ....
- ....
- ....
- ....
- ....
- ....
- ....
- ....

- ....
- ....
- ....
- ....
- ....
- ....
- ....
- ....

Directions:

....
....
....
....
....
....
....
....
....
....
....
....
....
....

Preparation Time: **Servings:**

RECIPE #16

RECIPE: _____

Ingredients:

- • ....
- • ....
- • ....
- • ....
- • ....
- • ....
- • ....
- • ....

- • ....
- • ....
- • ....
- • ....
- • ....
- • ....
- • ....
- • ....

Directions:

....

....

....

....

....

....

....

....

....

....

....

....

....

....

....

Preparation Time: **Servings:**

RECIPE #17

RECIPE: _____

Ingredients:

- ....
- ....
- ....
- ....
- ....
- ....
- ....
- ....

- ....
- ....
- ....
- ....
- ....
- ....
- ....
- ....

Directions:

....

....

....

....

....

....

....

....

....

....

....

....

....

....

....

Preparation Time: **Servings:**

RECIPE #18

RECIPE: _____

Ingredients:

- ....
- ....
- ....
- ....
- ....
- ....
- ....
- ....

- ....
- ....
- ....
- ....
- ....
- ....
- ....
- ....

Directions:

....

....

....

....

....

....

....

....

....

....

....

....

....

....

....

Preparation Time: **Servings:**

RECIPE #19

RECIPE: _____

Ingredients:

- ....
- ....
- ....
- ....
- ....
- ....
- ....
- ....

- ....
- ....
- ....
- ....
- ....
- ....
- ....
- ....

Directions:

....
....
....
....
....
....
....
....
....
....
....
....
....
....

Preparation Time: **Servings:**

RECIPE #20

RECIPE: _____

Ingredients:

- ....
- ....
- ....
- ....
- ....
- ....
- ....
- ....

- ....
- ....
- ....
- ....
- ....
- ....
- ....

Directions:

....

....

....

....

....

....

....

....

....

....

....

....

....

....

....

Preparation Time: **Servings:**

ABOUT THE AUTHOR

Jason Scotts loves to explore new things which has led him to making his home brewed beer. He is a writer of many books, he writes mainly from a personal perspective and out of experience with added straightforward facts that has helped build the foundations of his books. Home brewing is one of his most loved passions apart from computers and fitness.

With his many books, he has helped many individuals reach their goals in various aspects of life. He writes various topics for all ages.

CPSIA information can be obtained
at www.ICGtesting.com
Printed in the USA
LVOW01s2317230916

505971LV00020B/563/P